# Life's Stink and Honey

Lynn Valentine

**Cinnamon Press**
:: small miracles from distinctive voices ::

Published by Cinnamon Press
www.cinnamonpress.com

The right of Lynn Valentine to be identified as author of this work has been asserted by her in accordance with the Copyright, Designs and Patent Act, 1988. © 2021, Lynn Valentine

ISBN 978-1-78864-125-8

British Library Cataloguing in Publication Data. A CIP record for this book can be obtained from the British Library.

All rights reserved. No part of this publication may be reproduced, stored in a retrieval system, or transmitted in any form or by any means, electronic, mechanical, photocopying, recording or otherwise without the prior written permission of the publishers. This book may not be lent, hired out, resold or otherwise disposed of by way of trade in any form of binding or cover other than that in which it is published, without the prior consent of the publishers.

Designed and typeset in Bodoni by Cinnamon Press. Cover design by Adam Craig.

Cinnamon Press is represented by Inpress

.

# Acknowledgements

Versions of some of these poems have previously been published. Thanks to the editors of *192 Magazine, Anti-Heroin Chic, Atrium, The Beach Hut, Barren Magazine, Black Bough Poetry, Broken Spine Arts, The Blue Nib, Dreich, Island Review, Nitrogen House, Northwords Now* and *Poetry Scotland*. Some of the Scots language poems were published by Hedgehog Poetry Press in my Scots pamphlet *A Glimmer o Stars*, published after winning the Hedgehog Poetry Press dialect competition in 2020. 'The Aunties' was commissioned by the Scottish Poetry Library's guest curator Aoife Lyall as part of the Scottish Poetry Library's Champions project in 2020. 'Some Just Call it the A9' was published in Scottish Writers Centre's *Borders and Boundaries* chapbook. 'The Clootie Well' was published in The Federation of Writers Scotland/New Voices Press anthology *Surfing*. 'The woman who fell in love with the sea' was published in The Federation of Writers Scotland/New Voices Press anthology *Sea Change*. 'Hellebores' featured in the Poetry in Public Places initiative run by WEA/Women in the Highlands. 'The Loast Bairn' was runner up in the Scots category of the Wigtown Poetry Prize 2021. 'April in Harris' won Highland Lit's poetry competition 2021.

Thanks to all the poetry encouragers especially my wonderful husband Calum; my amazing siblings—The Bairns—Jenny, Diane and Jim; my fabulous Cinnamon Press mentor, Jay Whittaker, from whom I learned so much; Donny O'Rourke and his brilliant bunch of Barrington Bards; Mark Davidson at Hedgehog Poetry Press and his merry array of Hoglets; The No-Name Poets—Anne Hay, Thomas Stewart and Olive M Ritch; Aoife Lyall; John Glenday; Wendy Pratt; Jim Mackintosh; Charlie Gracie; Hamish MacDonald; Damien Donnelly; Gaynor Kane; Matthew MC Smith at Black Bough Poetry and his Top Tweet Tuesday gang; The Federation of Writers Scotland; The Whickering Girls; Black Isle Writers' Group; Angus; Yvonne; Alan; Karen V and Elspeth. Ta to my canine companions Flo and Marag, who have listened to these poems without judgement and kept me company whilst I was writing. Huge thanks to Jan at Cinnamon Press who believed in these poems and awarded me the Cinnamon Literature prize in 2020, leading to the publication of this book.

# Contents

| | |
|---|---|
| A Flourish of Sun | 11 |
| The Cleaners | 12 |
| Some just call it the A9 | 13 |
| The Nightwatchman | 14 |
| Clothed in Soft Raiment | 15 |
| There Must Be Other Words for Crow | 16 |
| Sheela Na Gig, Rodel | 17 |
| Winter Night | 18 |
| Suicidal Thoughts of Deer | 19 |
| Thi Leid o Hame | 20 |
| Junk Drawer Day | 21 |
| Recovery takes a Decade | 22 |
| Born in the slums | 23 |
| The Aunties | 24 |
| Easdale Island | 25 |
| The Clootie Well | 26 |
| Form of a Hare | 27 |
| Sister Horse | 28 |
| Caring for Shrimps | 29 |
| Laundry Day | 30 |
| Lacuna | 31 |
| Conversation with Walter Benjamin on Angelus Novus | 32 |
| Gloamin | 33 |
| In a Glasgow library, 1987 | 34 |
| Thi Loast Bairn | 35 |
| The woman who fell in love with the sea | 36 |
| That Morning | 37 |
| Navigating the small hours | 38 |
| waterfall | 39 |
| Alone in Iona Abbey | 40 |
| What Happens When a Child Leaves Home | 41 |
| My Mother's Complaint | 42 |
| Winter Solstice Haibun at the Lhanbryde Standing Stones | 43 |
| Trick | 44 |
| We Lose the South | 45 |
| Ma faither at fower a.m. | 46 |
| Grief as an Iceberg | 47 |
| A Museum Piece | 48 |
| All That is Needed | 49 |
| Following the River Tay | 50 |

| | |
|---|---|
| An Elephant Never Forgets | 51 |
| Landscaper | 52 |
| The Kitchen Floor | 53 |
| April in Harris | 54 |
| Genetics of Depression | 55 |
| A hop, A skip, A jump | 56 |
| At Hallgrimskirkja | 57 |
| Witness | 58 |
| Rag Dollies | 59 |
| On Birsay Causeway | 60 |
| Painted Ladies Rapture | 61 |
| At Culbin Sands | 62 |
| In August | 63 |
| Winter Soup | 64 |
| The Magic Lantern | 65 |
| A Loast Freen | 66 |
| The Funeral Celebrant takes on Difficult Times | 67 |
| Hellebores | 68 |

For C and the Bairns

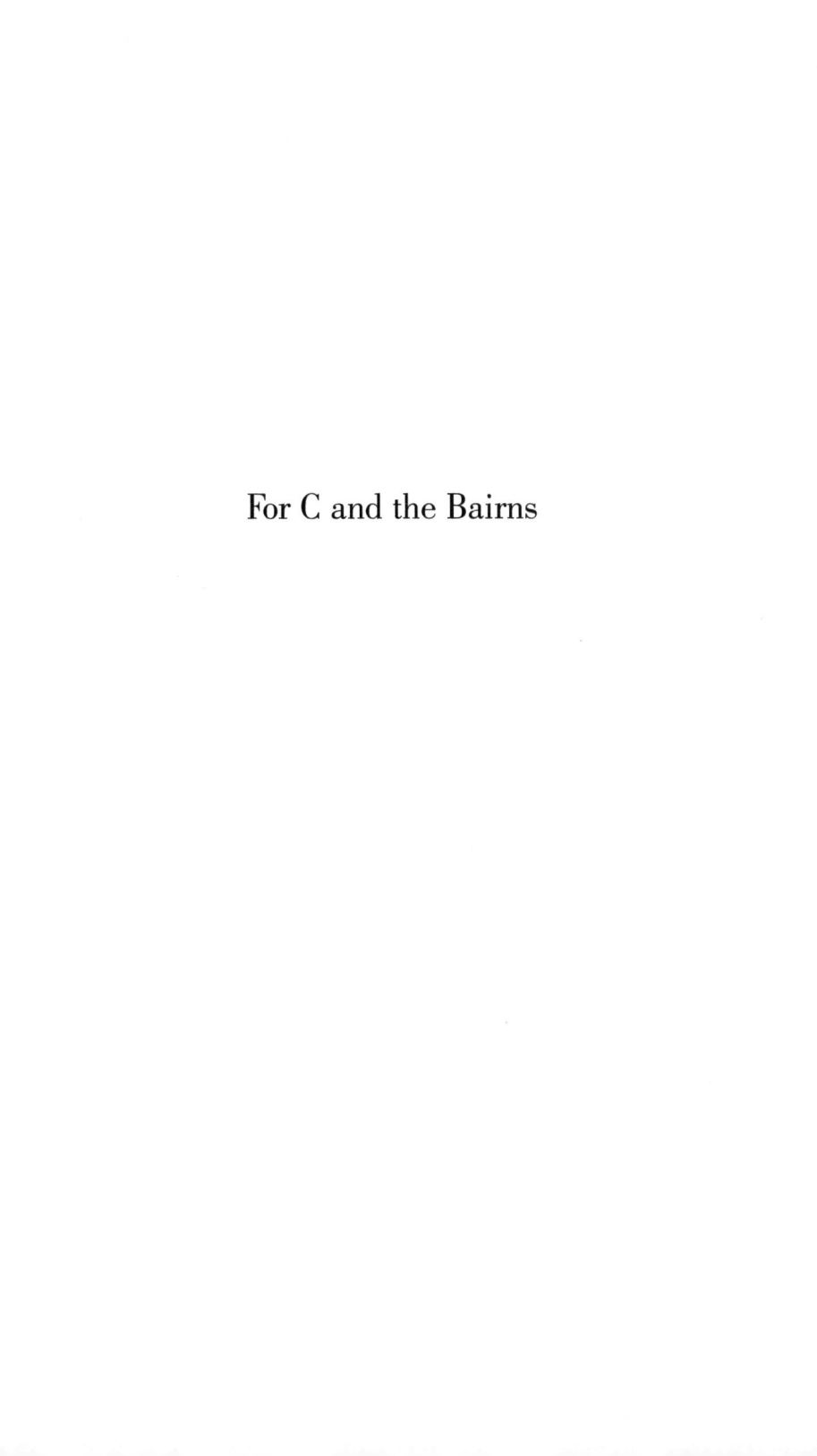

# Life's Stink and Honey

# A Flourish of Sun

Midsummer a surprise to those who have handled the weight of winter,
they flop in shorts sold at *The Factory Shop* for a fiver,
milk-pretty legs thin in this world of burning and cups of pale rum.

Heat peels roofs back, shifts into rooms where snow used to drift.
Dogs circle unsatisfactory trees, mongrels mad with lack of shade,
long grass pulped to dust. All night, light syrups in at the windows.

Bees can't hold a waggle dance, are confused, too slow.
Blue roses swoon, futile in remembrance of rain.
You ask – *Did you forget to take your pills again?*

I am awake every hour, the bright orange fizz in my brain.
I am light as a wren. I wonder if I'll return to winter –
to a seam of frost, to the half-shut moon, fat lap of dark.

# The Cleaners

*after Wislawa Szymborska*

Some unknown people dust the world,
mop round after tragedies, offer
a clear river, a green park,
somewhere fresh to sit and think.

My Dad, a council man,
minimum wage, clearing roadside drains,
other people's silt and shit.

I knew the name of Weil's disease
when I was small, would worry on it,
survey Dad for a sweaty brow,
an unlikely cough.

Some days he'd come back pale:

the man after the accident,
the man after the ambulance,
the man after the police had gone,

the man who would damp
down blood, throw down sand,
lift gristle up in both his hands.

# Some just call it the A9

*a visit to a dying mother*

There is a road
streaked with longing,
a thief of sorts, where
a Red Kite cries
for scraps of heart meat.

You stop the car,
say take what you want,
rest your body
on the border.
*111 miles to Perth*
reads the sign, then beyond.

A startle of antlers
flares in the string of trees
at the layby,
small stag running,
daring you to make
more of this long road.

## The Nightwatchman

I worked night-shift as a child,
guided my sister back to bed.
I slept lightly, always on the job,
scared to sleep in case I missed her toy owl's
floor thump, the soft sigh of springs
as Diane raised herself like Lazarus,
rolled forward into the night, feet
feathering the floor. I watched her
blank stare fix upon the midnight window.
My whisper sliced the air,
*Diane come back to me.*

Some nights she'd head for the stairs,
nightdress trailing like angel wings.
I'd guide her from her flight, lead her
past the sharp contours of the cabinet
that perched in the hall, corners
primed to catch a too-fast child
or those that did not care if cut.
*Diane come back to your bed.*

As an adult I slept soundly,
work over, sister in another town.
Too far away when others saved her
with a blue light's flash in the black.
There will be future nights
when she turns to the dark,
when sleep-walking will seem
like a good idea. I will my thoughts
southwards, tack my heart to her door.
Night-shift begins again,
*sister I'm here.*

## Clothed in Soft Raiment

The house at Benderloch
wore suits instead of ivy, coats
where Virginia Creeper should have been.
I never knew why this man desired
his jackets to be lacquered dark by rain.

I imagined him, night's work, the pinning
of a pair of trousers where a trellis
should have held a rose or runner beans.
Sweat seeping—unpacking his wardrobe—
life's stockpile—hanging like broken trees.

# There Must Be Other Words for Crow

High trees
a flap of shadow   wing

My sister hooded
my father as raven

Darkness
you in their grip

Beaks bearing weight
more   than they can hold

You   spitting feathers up
spreading claws   to face west

A shrinking from   human form
a black budding   in your breast

I see you shining   flying
bringing   twig   stone
seaweed   to the nest

# Sheela Na Gig, Rodel

Such a long road to drive.
I find you weathered by Harris winds,
worn in the smirr of rain,
hollowed, unholy mother.

I seek your protection, projection
of fertility, one stopped hand
holding a child or a lamb;
the other lost in a shape
that meant something once.

My barren belly
concaves in the wet
afternoon, my waterproof
the only second skin I'll own.

Yet there's hope in your arms,
the cleft in your legs, an open
                    O
on the rough bricks of stone.

# Winter Night

*after Boris Pasternak*

This year we are selling books
to buy bread. What can I part with?
The signed scribbled Ginsberg?
The frailty of an old family bible?
Perhaps my mother's copy of Doctor Zhivago?

I misremember, there's space on the shelf,
she may have only watched the film.
This miracle—witnessing her sit—
transfixed at the tale of Sharif and Christie,
while dinner slumped forgotten, unnoticed.

Unnoticed dinners are rare now. We choose
to go hungry, take a third cup of weak
tea while children eat. Mothers stand
in the church shop, food vouchers scrunched
down in purses, those purses blush-red with shame.

What to buy? Pasta, milk, tins, a sweetie
hidden for the middle one's birthday
next week. Mothers so grateful to the man
behind the counter, he is my father who once
had a wife who loved Doctor Zhivago.

## Suicidal Thoughts of Deer

A stag runs ahead at an angle,
hurt somewhere on the A835.
A car must have struck it, yet
the monarch turns, hurtles its
full flush of bulk towards me,
willing me and the Mini to finish

things off. I tell the stag—this car
is too small for you—too meagre
to give you what you want. Go rest
by the loch, coffin yourself
in water and moss. I'll meet you
there, leave this road.
You can ask if it matters
who's with you when you go.

# Thi Leid o Hame

*after Roger Robinson*

A hae cairriet this hansel withoot kennin,
this thrapple that thraws oot thi rrrs.
Fir years a thocht tae smoor it doon,

as teachers wid, eyewis thi correktions,
thi head instead o heid, thi dead instead
o deid. Ma faither gied it tae me,

ma granny tae—aa those who draggit
oan tae land at my hame toon—fish
who grew hurdies and settilt there.

A unpack the bag—it sings sangs o hame
an faimily an athin o the sea—thi reek
o Smokies that still maks ma veggie moo
slabber, thi lang cauld wind wheechin in

fae thi Flairs, thi reid o the cliffs bricht
at ony time o year. A will tak this hansel
an pass it oan, scrieve ma wurds, sing ma sangs.

## Junk Drawer Day

Snow wakes you
to remind you that you don't have children,
those out-of-date parsley seeds in the junk drawer
will never germinate.

You make coffee—sweet, bitter coffee—
this is not a metaphor for your life?
Your reflection grimaces at you
from the kitchen window,
you remember when you wore blue mascara,
had Japan on your wall.

And later, when the drawer kept a child's bracelet,
secret seeds of faith.
Somehow, you've taped all that up, made a magnet
of your heart for dogs, bees and postcards
from pals who you've not seen for years.

The pocket of your housecoat carries a Swiss army knife
in case you ever have to kill a man at 5.a.m.
or open a bottle of champagne
or snip winter kale for breakfast
when you're days away from being paid.

There's no need for shoe horns when you walk
in bare feet, when you are a martyr
to the frost, when your tongue catches
a drop of snow and you laugh like a child
for the child you never had.

## Recovery takes a Decade

In the wood, the Grizzly took me for her own.
Dressed me in the blood of others, added
mud and bone. I ran with her for ten
full seasons, pitched low in winter, a mirror
twinned in spring. We fed slim from river,
mapped the grass as graph paper, each blade,
each turn of stone. Like her, I could not climb trees,
find the bees' sweet honey that offered hopes of home.

# Born in the slums

She chose bright light
when there was dark,
refused to ever make
a mark against her
slum home.
She talked
of neighbours kind and poor
the laughter in amongst
the dour,
hardly mentioned
her Mum away, Dad in the
army with little pay,
the doing without,
the outside loo,
bringing up her brothers too.
She said *times were hard
but I loved it there*
and in the meantime
said a prayer
for central heating,
kids with bellies,
three meals a day,
the colour telly,
prawn cocktail crisps
from the ice-cream van
and fish and chips on Friday.

# The Aunties

They had the gift. Hidden about them
like a penny at the bottom of a pocket.

But theirs was a silver coin. On high days
they flattened your hand, palm up and

snap, out of their mouths flowed planets
and stars, life's stink and honey, babies

being born, relationships stalling, illnesses
yet to come. Never a date of death,

only a hint of feather, of crow. I laughed
as a child, thought them witches, hoodwinkers.

Now the crow cracks the glass, the moon turns her head,
the evening thickens with visions from aunts long-dead.

# Easdale Island

I dreamt of the village
on fetid London streets,
bees drowning in foxglove bells,
flooded quarries overspill,
perfume of salt and old stone.

Memory of hands pressing on slate,
a claim on broken houses as my own.

On these city roads I walk
the way I did back then, balance
the fall of water on either side,
dizzy with want for the rough touch
of grass on my feet, the call of a northerly storm.

# The Clootie Well

We knottit oor wishes roon thi well,
tyit them a tae thi trees, white fir a bairn,
blue fir a cuir. Wir nervish gaggles
ringin at corbies croakin in thi auld oaks.

Nane grantit, nane lastit, thi reid
runnin, the blackness takin ower
us baith. You awa by simmerdim,
me an ma belly emptie.

Noo they're clearin thi woods,
takin awa thi sheets, thi cloots,
even a pair o drawers.
A think thi last wid mak ye laugh.

A wish a could still ca ye Mither,
see yir heid turn roon at ma call,
some grey efternuins I dauner,
echo yir name intae thi well.

## Form of a Hare

Born in the form, eyes open
to the puzzle of Spring;
crossings of light,
lanterns of grass. Fur
a small cover against storms.

So much loss this year
as we walk the fields,
searching for leverets,
blazes of pheasants.

You still frail, arm threaded
in mine, feet still finding
their place. We spy
feathers of fieldfares,
ancient pathways of hares.

The shape of rain fastened
in faraway trees.

# Sister Horse

I never knew how high a horse could be,
  Calesca, the steam rising off her back
    the way a small kettle can fill a kitchen
      with a sudden mist of rain. A Chestnut
        with firelit hooves, that smoored through
          Welsh grass and moss, presented
            to both of us. Your turn first.

Your breath steady, hands to match,
  up and on to meet your catch of the day.
    Something kindred spurred her on,
      her recognition of a spirit—wilful,
        wind-bitten—free, then the galloping,
          the laughing, the fear that crossed
            my face as I watched you sister with
              your sister horse unwinding in the breeze.

## Caring for Shrimps

Remember that time we tried to grow sea monkeys?
Shook them out of their packet into tap-water.
None of them thrived yet here I am free-diving,
wheezing lungs repaired in the Ventolin blue of sea.

I find those monkeys alongside things I'd lost for years.

Remember the time we tried to make babies?
I bundle them up but they're too slippery
to hold and I can't carry the sea.

Remember the time we cast Mum's ashes?
She's here with Granny, they're taking care
of all of the ocean.

Remember the time I walked into salt water?
Never looking back until I managed to swim to shore?
That version of me is here—looking after the babies and sea monkeys.

# Laundry Day

Barefoot we stood, heads touching

        hands together, a kiss of cloth.

                Then out again, a kind of dance

        til' all was done, no kisses left.

Only a brush of cool in the night,

            the tuck of your absent hands.

# Lacuna

Your fingers
unravel the quilt,
your tears pearl the bed.

Just imagine if he wasn't a box
in the spare room,
wasn't a photo in the hall.

He's moved east with you,
he's down at the beach
but haar obscures the view.

You heat the hob,
spooning coffee from the can
you bought in Prague.

That whole street filled
with your favourite things.

Bundles of wool, shelves of tins,
the café where you drank tea
steeped green with peppermint leaves.

Hope was measured in small things.

Now you drink coffee alone,
forgo the sweetness of sugar,
the thickness of cream.

And you weave, shuttle
and loom, knot traps
for other people's dreams.

# Conversation with Walter Benjamin on *Angelus Novus*

This angel that follows you, cannot be stopped,
will not drop the wings of history. I am reading
Forché today, Forché always. She stands witness,
holds onto the tail of the angel in her hands.
Is Klee with you tonight, is the angel wailing?
If I tell you the last time I saw Forché on stage
was March 2020, this *Lateness of the World*
being birthed into being. Would you believe
what has happened since then? Was it like that for you?
A chasm of months crushed to a life of sorrow.
We light beacons on the hill that we might speak
with neighbours. No-one comes, the fire goes out.
Charcoal ghosts leave only shadows and holes.
Where is the angel? Will you send light?

# Gloamin

And you look out the window
and look   really look
the mountains low
still snowed   hunkered
into winter still

the sky high
the everlasting orange and blue

And you think
this is why

This   This

# In a Glasgow library, 1987

They borrow six Mills and Boons at a time,
maximum limit, hover at the door,
wait while I'm classifying new arrivals.
How many books does it take to chip
away the grey of the council estate?

I stick a small rose on the spines
to be filed under Romance,
no symbol for sex so the Harlequins
nuzzle suggestively next
to tales of love and heroines.

The Zane Greys and the like
are filed with the sign of a gun.
I'd prefer a horse if I'm honest,
likewise with daggers for crime,
a swap for the O of a magnifying glass.

This estate is commonplace
for knives, the odd gun, the odd death,
hardmen, violence, the government sucking it dry.
I'm grateful to those who order new roses,
happy for those who travel with horses.

# Thi Loast Bairn

Thair ir meenits ma dochter wull wauk mi
in thi nicht wi hir girnin; a loup roon the room
an roon agin, girnin fir the mither wha couldnae

let hir see licht, couldnae let hir be born
Is this a tod then, a vixen circlin thi yaird?
A Reid Kite blawn aff coorse intae derkness?

A pit ma fist in ma moo tae stoap ma shriekin.

A wullnae blait like a sheepie fir a lamb—
wullnae own ma voice fir air thit's ower shairp—
fir blank stanes aneath snaw.

# The woman who fell in love with the sea

I married the sea    for too long
    I'd hidden from her   land-locked
          in cities where rivers died
   for lack of salt and tides

        she'd missed me but had gifted
her kiss of spume to other lovers

        New Year's Day   rough   hungover
          her tears   at last   twinned with mine

she marked me with a slap
        as I dived   barefoot and broken
   a jolt of cold   then acceptance
      my breath   a pearl   a severed shell

          kick on   kick out   clutch the horizon
                swim   swim   again

# That Morning
*for Joe*

Everything still, glazed clouds like an oil painting
smeared too thick, the river set with varnish—currents
hushed—passers-by not passing, watching the hearse.

Even the horses knew where to stand in the pasture,
heads arched, not a whinny or a glance.

Only the sleekness of that long black car—
you the only one on the move—the slow creep
along the village street to join the stones of the silent.

# Navigating the small hours

One: another of those nights netted in
    wakefulness, each minute filleted into silence.

Two: a shoal of bad thoughts flood
    from the walls, the room and I unmoored in their flux.

Three: up and out, a grand march of stars
    dredge the dark, red fret of Merry Dancers.

Four: returning to land, the bliss of you
    seeping heat like a stolen month of summer.

Five: rust ship of night filed down,
    dawn birthed from the firth, smooth, quiet.

## waterfall

      morning rain chases tourists
               away
just us in the loch   mist-slip of moisture
on hair & skin          me   you
         all else forgotten

for that hour we shape ourselves to water
     loch bodies   rain   bodies   loch
          more  salmon or seal
        everything other

        becoming water
       water  becoming us


             noon—we catch up with tourists
sit outside the green-stepped café
drink tea & scroll our phones


          hundreds   more dead   no end to it
i scour my damp hair down to feel
my skull                  remove
      last drops of water

# Alone in Iona Abbey

I thought I felt his breath there,
an opening
in my palms, while tourists knelt outside
bothering graves.

Was it just a dance of wind
through a worn door,
a chance of sunlight and shadow as I
prayed?

Since then I've been watchful,
quote half-forgotten
Sunday school blessings, prime
myself for signs:

dark skies smoking blood in a place
far away,
the sea salting claims on what's mine.

## What Happens When a Child Leaves Home

Their shoes lie like dead dogs in the hall,
food rots like rabbits with myxomatosis.

Fingerprint paintings could be fish in a bowl,
swirling in a two-minute memory of home.

A forgotten coat hangs like Mrs Black's cat,
when the boys killed it and called her witch.

A toothbrush in the shape of a bear, furs
in the holiday washbag. All of this

happened—none of this happened—we still wait
on cows coming home, trampling the grass to the door.

## My Mother's Complaint

*You're so far up the map now, I never know where to look to find the weather at yours.*

Each time her children moved, my mother
tacked her heart to the TV weather map.

Imagined her offspring in autumn coats
or shivering in the chill after the six o'clock news.

Weighted the places where she could find us,
tethered and tied us to her coordinates,

located her son in the centre of things, held
my sisters' summers in the same spot as hers.

Mum, think if Scotland had a face, find the eye
where two firths meet and gild your love upon it.

I'll still find you when the chart grows dark
with only time and weather left to bind us.

# Winter Solstice Haibun
## at the Lhanbryde Standing Stones

They try to catch the angle—white sun bowing low in the afternoon—but the stones have moved or the world has tilted a little since their construction. Maybe the stones have been loosened by moles, blind miners, tunnelling excavations to eternity; maybe undercut by the farmer as he ploughs the field each second spring, cursing the turns he has to make because of archaeology.

No light aligns where it should, in the middle of winter's prism. How hard they try to set the sun with stones—repositioning their bodies, placing planets with pinched fingers—lying raggedy on the cold bright field.

*All is stone and snow;*
*light won't bend to perfection,*
*carry it with you*

# Trick

I was the child who would catch flies in mid-air—
their journey stopped by my fingers— my hand
a safe place to land. I did not harm them, never
wished them ill, they'd be released at the door,
going about their business still. Can I catch flies
in middle-aged hands? Can I stop that bullet
for you, Penn and Teller style? Blood bouncing,
guns primed, me—open-handed, open-mouthed.

I try to halt it any which way, the stage dressed
in theatrical red, a flash of black in the wings.
My senses are lightning, hurricanes,
veins of hot rain, the lull of something
that might turn into grief, might yet
turn into the greatest show on earth.

## We Lose the South

with a gaggle of road-weary cyclists,
posing for photos at the top of the land.

Ahead lie rumbling currents, dark feathers
of wind gathering foot passengers in.

The crossing is short, fulmars follow
the boat roll, the grey grumble of sea.

Set down, we see butter-rich fields, countless
fat cows the colour of darkest cream.

We stroll on beaches as tides suck at gaps
in conversation, shells are picked like strawberries.

Midnight stumbles in with hardly a change
in the air. We sit, punch-drunk on light.

## Ma faither at fower a.m.

Mornins, ma faither whustled
as if the wurld wis his alane,
his lang stravaig thru snaw tae thi yaird
mindit by thi big reid tod an thi squaikin spuggies.

We dreamit o Dad,
thi suddent sneeze o a snawploo
chairgin tae life in his hauns.
His canny handlin o a fauchled toon

as he clearit thi streets, tried no tae
rouse the sleepers, the fidgetin bairns,
fowk bundilt in their jammies,
their furst quiet coffee o the day.

Aifter, busses an cars set oot
ontae noo-safe streets, we makit
snaw-bas fae the slush pylit up,
ma Da deid tae us as he snorit on tae denner.

## Grief as an Iceberg

You get used to it, these ships of ice
sailing past the door, there will be another
before too long. A flock of tourists perch,
unnatural in their summer clothes, oohing
and aahing. Some bring food, some share,
*we used to live in Iceberg Alley too.*

You get used to it, like kisses on the mouth,
like your first rainbow as a child, the sight
of the Northern Lights on that holiday long ago.
Have you ever heard an iceberg break?
The long creak into the sea, keening,
screaming, as it tries to keep itself whole.

# A Museum Piece

That summer she became a stone;
rigid obsidian fixed in the museum case.

For years she was lava—hot and strong—
then she hardened, compressed, cooled.

And she waited for someone to raise her
but the doctors locked her up,

labelled her incorrectly, catalogued
her with the wrong tools. No air

in the exhibit box, no fire to set her free.
She was looked at, handled, remarked on,

her pebbled life in the hands of others,
a pounding into grit.

She learned to lie, to display herself,
to etch a different story on the glass.

That summer she smashed the case—
rolled herself upwards—home.

## All That is Needed

When I am alone I will turn eastwards
to live in a brown house at the edge of the sea.
I will inherit storm-cracked apple trees
and the wild goats that crop their meals
close to the shore where the green boat sleeps.

I will eat cheese as fat as the cheeks
of the moon and pare the good red apples
as thin as fingernails with no-one to complain.
I will drink sour wine saved from a communion years ago,
and wash it down with water drawn from somewhere secret.

I will not cook and no-one will ask me to.
I will buy bread from the grocer's van
once a week along with tins that open easily.
I will leave the fish alone, unbothered by a hook,
and if someone visits accidentally I will ask that intruder to go.

I will watch my face grow pursed and thin in the mirror
of the stream while my hair grows thick
as brambles. I will turn pebbles to find precious little.
I will stuff my mouth with sun when it's hot,
and on cold mornings I will ask the tide for answers.

# Following the River Tay

River chimes her long rhyme from hill
to horizon. A chink of notes on Ben Lui,
an orchestral roar as she meets the sea.

Populations grow, press onto her shores,
she could swallow them all if she wanted.

Ancestors fished from her darkened limbs,
my grandfather swam in her star-filled arms.

She thought to shoal my brother in his boat,
open her throat for her own water child.

Grey seals guard the bridge, messengers
between this world and the next.

My mum swore she could hear water
from the window of her hospice room
river to ocean.

## An Elephant Never Forgets

They move through snap of dry grass,
ruminate on the state of the plains.
My mother stretches her long trunk, tickles
my niece's head, urges her to keep up.

In the herd a sister here and there,
nurtured since birth or just by love.
They snuffle, snort, strip leaves from trees,
scream with glee or fear.

All ears flap towards the matriarch.

And when she sinks on hobbled knees,
her wise grey face cancelled out,
the elephants link trunk-to-tail,
try soldering their broken chain.

# Landscaper

His work, the slow heaping
of soil into a grave.
He digs the shape of a life,
stands well back while mourners
seed the ground with tears.

Afterwards, a nod to his mate,
the push of earth against wood and air,
the filling in, the flattening.

In summer he tends the flower beds,
talks to roses, watches
each pale petal fall.

# The Kitchen Floor

*after Donika Kelly*

You are a floor where cockroaches gather
in the last of the light, where crumbs fall
and you receive them. There is a rug that sits
on top of you, covering you in all the wrong places.
There is milk spilled and never wiped away.
There is a doormat inset into your tiles.
There are scratches on you where your man had sex
with someone else. You are pliant vinyl with glue
unsticking, a red and black chequered mess.
Everyone steps on you without taking off their shoes,
their dirt sticks to you and they refuse to brush.
Hard wooden chairs take root; a table dominates
your space. Crows call from garden pines,
moles burrow under the house.
You shift, you move, you want to be ceiling
or air— even wallpaper—you remain floor.

## April in Harris

Bog-soaked on Clisham, joking about lightning,
we're the highest beings in the Outer Hebrides.

Not Paris this, our jackets not the latest in French
chic but suited to sitting on a hill, sharing a peece.

Would you rather sip a brandy under a striped awning's
shade of a Parisian café? Or feel the warmth
of Heinz Cream of Tomato on your chapped lips?

And the pedestrians are crows and hares, beetles,
an eagle if we're blessed. And the sun comes out for just a turn.

And the lochans line up—an emerald necklace fit for a lover.
And the land ripens with gold-soaked light.
Cold air hangs between us—we drink and drink.

# Genetics of Depression

The bees came to me in that sweat-hell sleep
after the first vaccination, they wanted me to tell them
but I wouldn't—I'm not giving you up—I refuse
to carry that stick to the hive. So it's me and the bees
in this half-land of headaches waiting for the week to be done.

The brim of sky makes my brain tear,
even the weather is undecided; a yellow apple of sun
squatted on the sea at 6 a.m. and now the mist is in,
cobwebbing everything. Did our ancestors lay themselves out
for sky burials of their own choosing? Did sisters go together?
Did they have bees to tell?

# A hop, A skip, A jump

Gran carried you to the sea,
a push in the fluid of her womb,
tip-toed slip of seaweed,
grit-red sandstone.

Ocean-cold, her feet placed
for a minute, just enough
to feel the pitch
of ice-sharp water,
a salt lick, undertow.

Later you'd do the same.
Buoy me up in currents
of your own making,
keep me from the snag
of tides, the flood of foam.

## At Hallgrimskirkja

I'm there again under a cool stone roof, my
doppelganger *Hildasdottir* sipping *kaffi* after
service, saying *hallo* to replicas of herself -
faces of blue eyes, upward-slanted cheeks.

I imagine myself tied to Magnus, Jon or Margret,
a belly drumming under my best woollen jumper,
the flush of newly-wed love snug inside.

Later we stroll down shuttered streets,
snigger at tourists as they stagger from boats -
sick after eating shark, watching whales.

We head home in the jeep, over ice-fields
and lava, past lagoons that shine too bright a blue.
We tend to the horses, eat cinnamon buns,
pretend that this island is real.

## Witness

Death is not what I thought it would be—
slow progression of doctors, bed and peace.

I hold her hand, can't let go,
can't ring the bell to let others know.

Tough all her life before this illness gripped her,
increasingly weaker 'til this quarter-hour fight.

A curl of strong fingers, her fury at leaving,
a grasp for my hand like a new-born child.

A wild colt galloping in the corral of her bed,
the mattress her saddle, the blankets her fence.

# Rag Dollies

A winter day spent hunkered
is she cuts screeds fae an auld saft sheet,
hauds peens in hir peelie lips,
tries tae keep thi scarlit in.

Thi shadda o bodies lain oot
ready fir hir hauns canny stitchin,
thi tick o work an quiet,
thi lack o a machine's whurr.

This streetch o linin wull mak seeven ir mair;
ainly she his thi knack o meisurement—
thi pattern mappit in hir heid – a frull o skirt,
a bonnie bunnit, thi broon velvet savit fir shin.

A hae nivir birthit a dolly, ma moo fu o peens,
a undae thi seam o thi livin fae thi deid.

# On Birsay Causeway

We weren't prepared, wore improper shoes,
the island half-sunk in fog. All the while,
the tide galloping—the planning we had
to do—how far to reach the landing light,
how long to touch improbable stones.

You trailed behind, unsure at first,
seaweed loose beneath your feet, water
welcoming a fall. By the time we arrived
we were knee-deep in sea muck but
gripped the rocks with blue-cold hands,
stepped shakily out onto new-old land.

## Painted Ladies Rapture

Better than the butterfly house,
this rush of colour you've brought to the north,
porphyry of thistles resolved into a burning bush.

I worship at your altar, *burned but not consumed*,
offer a prayer for your laced fretwork, silent
as your flames scorch across the garden.

## At Culbin Sands

A walk, something to take our minds off it.

A wood gives way to sand gives way
to far-off sea. And suddenly
we are in a forest of splinters

and hag forms, dead trees petrified.
Some shout, arms raised, others turn
inwards cradling babies made from sand.

My voice gives way to pain,
a bar-tailed godwit puddles in what's left
of the surf, finds a meal.

# In August

I gave myself to heat,
to barley bubbling in the fields,
to fat lambs being separated
from months of mothering.

I wheezed blossomed air,
cheered the bees
as they stole their last drop of pollen
from the rose hedge.

I watched the moths
in their ecstasy of slaughter,
their *Danse Macabre*
in the dusky porch light.

I joined the chatter
of house martins, writing
their goodbyes, zebra-ing
the sky, until all was wing.

# Winter Soup

Heating borscht while the snow hits,
makes me think I'm a bit-player
in a Russian novel; the fat cook
or the mother who has to eke the last
of the beets to feed her hungry girls.

But I set the table for two only,
blue bowls from Crail, the wedding spoons.
I catch the solstice in my hands,
pass it to you. There will be light again
on both of us; and gently falling snow.

# The Magic Lantern

*after T.S. Eliot*

Let us stay now, you and I, in the wise light
of Leicester Square tube station, let's preserve
our first kiss among crowds, nose-wrinkling smells,
the hiss of London fading, a blur of colours whirling.

I remember red the best—the shine of love
being birthed in the most ordinary of places.
You boarded North, I boarded West — all the way
to Hammersmith I lingered on that question of a kiss,

Would you be my one steady love, would others
come and go? I take tea with flatmates, swither
with indecision. a phone call's hope clogging
up my thoughts. Do I dare contact you first?

Thirty years disappear. I kiss you
in the kitchen, think of Leicester Square.

## A Loast Freen

Thi sma snaw o the lambs is later than iver this year,
thi Mey's near oot, daffies are droonin in rattlestanes.
Thi spuggies hae bairns—cauld bairns.
A've taen tae pokin the dugs moltins intae trees
tae waarm the nests, am waatchin oot fir foggie bummers tae.

An a wunner whaur ye are noo—ir ye facin thi blast
o winter still—sleekit winds startin low then takin ower
thi hail lenth o sky. Ir is it sweet whaur yi are,
a strawberry sun lichtin yir path? Is thir still time to mak
oor peace, tak a jig thegither, haud ane anither in sma snaw?

## The Funeral Celebrant takes on Difficult Times

Let me take you sister, sit you down
on Mum's bench, share a flask of tea,
break open a pack of your favourite sweets.

Are you tired from dealing in the dead?
Reciting a poem, the last kind words?
All the words that bring happy tears.

A life lived...

Two funerals a day, ten or more a week.
Busy, busy, the family joke that you can't
sit still, *hae a gless erse*, comes true.

Let me sit you down sister,
offer you chocolate, small
gossip of the living
and never-ending cups of tea.

# Hellebores

How can these aliens exist
in a northern winter, sprawling flesh
in an empty bed, marinating in thin,
harsh earth. Each wax-eared petal
metalled to the soil. Yet if I lift
their heads, they listen
for unbroken light, a travelling sky.

Lightning Source UK Ltd.
Milton Keynes UK
UKHW041300020322
399460UK00008B/120